The Love and Resentment I Hold

Ori Sentiments

BookLeaf Publishing

India | USA | UK

Presentation by *BookLeaf Publishing*

Web: www.bookleafpub.com

E-mail: info@bookleafpub.com

ISBN: 9789358312492

First edition 2023

Trigger Warning: The following poems
mention rape, sexual assault and harassment,
sexism and misogyny, eating disorders, and body
image issues.

Please engage in self-care if you
decide to continue reading.

Conditional Love, Misplaced Pride, and the Pointless Pursuit of Approval

"I'm proud of you and the person
you've become."

These words are written in birthday cards
and sound distant through phone calls
They're mentioned casually over breakfast,
spelled out on my waffle with whipped cream
at the diner my father and his father
take me to every Saturday
It's sentimentally reassured
when my uncertain future is brought up… often

Coming from family,
that sentence should probably mean more to me
I hear it a lot,
though I don't think I could ever appreciate it
the same way I did before
A phrase that used to make me feel
warm and happy
now feels more like a control tactic
used against me

"I'm proud of you."
These words squeeze
uncomfortably tight in my chest
They are a shadow I'm living in,
an expectation I need to live up to,
a warning not to fuck up,
to stay in line
because I know I'm not
the person they all think they're proud of,
not anymore

I'm hiding behind their projected pride and joy,
using it like a mask
because if they saw me without it,
they wouldn't even know me
Or maybe they would, but wouldn't want to

They would be so disappointed in
the person I really am now:
a person who quietly outgrew their mold,
who wordlessly slipped from
their tight hourglass grasp

Someone whose perspective has led them
to think differently than they were raised to
Whose morals and beliefs did not
stand the test of time
Whose faith was abandoned for
something a little less rickety,

a little less blind
Whose goals and ambitions never aligned
with the hopes passed along to them
like hand-me-downs that
never did fit quite right

I began to perform to keep earning pride that
didn't really belong to me
It was simple.
Just agree with them.
Nod.
Stay quiet.
Bite your tongue.
Never present authentically to those
that say they'd love you no matter what,
but could so easily be proved wrong
with masks ripped off and
glass ceilings shattered
because love and pride are conditional

Approval is dangled like a carrot on a stick,
held just out of my reach above my head
I run, ready to jump for it,
but I trip over the conditions of their love
before I can even take the leap
and land on my face
in the dirt that is their disappointment

A Letter to My 16 Year Old Self

You're figuring out how to touch, how to feel
from another's lips, from another's hands
only through breathless poetry and bolder art,
while other people your age are dating
and experiencing love for the first time

You and I both know
how much you hurt yourself
by romanticizing everything,
every accidental glance and brush of arms,
every kind word you mistake for interest,
every confusing feeling you have for a friend,
because you want these things
to mean more than they do
so badly and you get your hopes up

You haven't been shown what love is yet,
but you've taught yourself the pain
caused by the disappointment
of your own broken ideals
You don't believe you can ever have
what your peers do
because you have nothing to offer anyone, right?
You'll feel this self-inflicted heartbreak,

this emptiness and detachment for years
and I'm so sorry

You're scared that you'll end up alone
You're planning a future that
revolves around this fear
because you know it will be your reality
No one will ever settle for you
No one will ever make sacrifices
or compromises to be with you

You'll be happy to know
that you were wrong
You're going to find someone who adores you
and will happily compromise,
someone who reminds you very often that you're
more than enough
You're going to know romantic love
and it will be very worth the wait
It will be worth this devastating loneliness
and alienation you're feeling now

You aren't unlovable
You aren't broken
You are so deserving of love
You'll learn.

Relationship Hierarchies (my significant others)

Why are romantic, sexual relationships
valued more than
even one's relationship with themself
and why are they set on a higher pedestal
than any other kind of connection?
Why are we incomplete if we aren't in one?
Why do we accept that these relationships
are supposed to be the most important,
most central aspect of our lives?

It's unfair that we expect our partners to be
everything for us
They should be our other halves,
the sole person who can complete us perfectly
(Are we not whole people on our own?)
That's such an unrealistic and high demand
How can we ask someone to hold
infinite space, time, and energy for us,
to provide for our every need
when a support system should always be
more than one person?

I love my best friend like I love my partner
Both of these beautiful people

compliment me perfectly
(but neither *complete* me because
I am already whole;
that's an important distinction)
so why is the emotional intimacy that
I share with them any less significant than
the intimacy I share with him
just because of the titles which
categorize our relationships?
Friends. Lovers.
Both of these people are so important to me and
I'm so happy around them
I would go to the ends of the earth
for either of them

I'm generous with my affection
because there's an unlimited supply of it
I have a lot of love to give
I can stuff so much care in my heart
and there's more than enough room in it for
two close relationships
You downplay and belittle my connections
just because
an amatonormative, allonormative society
tells you that you should adhere to
relationship hierarchies,
but I love having
more than one significant other

Performative

I stumbled across porn too young,
but I learned how a woman
should look for a man
when she is under him,
pliant, arched, and open
I learned how she should sound
to make him feel
like he is doing a good job of pleasing her
even when he is rubbing her left labia
instead of her clit,
like he is trying to sand her down
until she molds to him
Ouch.

The Men that Assume Ownership of Me

I was taught early on that
I would never belong to myself

I've had my father's last name
since I took my first breath
*(All of my accomplishments
are tied to it,
like the credit of my hard work
doesn't belong to me at all.)*

Male teachers have policed my clothes
since elementary school
"Show me that your shorts are finger-tip length."
"Your tank top is distracting to boys."
*(I only wore long pants and
baggy tee-shirts for you for years…)*
I was quiet and 10, but already
a sexualized stumbling block,
made responsible for
keeping the rowdy, noisy boys who
I was assigned a seat next to
focused on their education,
while they got away with
passing me drawings of cartoon dicks,

tugging on my hair, and poking me
with sharpened pencils
to draw out my oh-so-amusing reactions
        (even though my shoulders
        were not the distraction.)
"Boys will be boys."
"They only tease you because they don't know
how to show you they have a crush on you."
        (Does that make it okay
        for you to touch me?
        Invade my space? Harass me?
        Did you think about how easily
        your behavior was excused back then
        when you sent unsolicited photos
        of your genitals last week
        or groped that pretty woman
        at the club last night?)

"No man will find you attractive
if you chop off all your hair."
My father said this to me,
as if I was supposed to care
        (Men don't spend an hour
        every morning styling my hair for me.
        Men don't have to deal with the
        weight and heat of it on my head.)
And when I finally did cut it all off,
an old man at my work told me I looked
"more serious and respectable."

(I wonder what connotations
he could have possibly
had with cropped hair
to make him say that to me.
I didn't ask for any man's
opinions on my appearance,
but was given many
over the course of my lifetime anyway.)

The myth of virginity determines my value
I'm only worth the cost of
the ring that was fitted onto my finger
before my hands
and my body
were even done growing
A promise of purity -
  (one I was never given
  a chance to make for myself) -
to the voyeuristic man in the sky
and to a hypothetical future husband
  (It's no surprise that I outgrew
  both the ring and that promise.)

Because no man will want chewed bubblegum,
or packing tape that picked up lint from
a tee-shirt and is no longer sticky,
or a chocolate bar that was
licked and rewrapped,
or an ineffective lock that

can be opened by many keys,
> *(I am not an object.)*
while a key that can open many locks is
somehow different, desirable
> *(How erect was your ego*
> *after being taught*
> *that your penis could ruin me?*
> *How thrilling was it for you to learn*
> *that I was new land for you*
> *to explore, conquer,*
> *and steal my most virtuous asset from*
> *like it was your God-given birthright?)*

But no man wants a total prude either
So stay untainted, but know exactly
how to please your husband
on your blood-stained wedding bed
A middle-aged man in the church
isolated me at 16 to deliver this message
and to make sure I knew
what a wife's duties were
"I would make a man happy someday."
> *(Is that the only way*
> *to make you happy?)*

I have my father's last name
until another man wants me to take his
The two become one
> *(You want to absorb*

and become my identity,
but you did not earn my degree
or the money in my bank account.
Why must I change
what everyone calls me
just because you feel like
I need a new title
that will show them you've
claimed fresh ownership over me?)

"There's no such thing as marital rape;
A woman belongs and submits to her husband."
    (Hearing my father rant
    about this entitlement when I was 12
    made me scared of marriage;
    A 22 year old asexual is still terrified
    about losing their right to say no.)
"It doesn't have to be good for you,
but it will be for him and
sometimes you just do what you have to do
to be a good spouse."
    (My heart hurts for my mother
    who said this to me once
    and for every other woman who
    is crushed by the weight of
    obligation and obedience,
    who were raised to believe
    they are owned by a man,
    but not owed

My hypothetical husband will want me
to have children for him
*(Remember when you sent me
that DM saying I look
submissive and breedable?
Men who write laws,
but wouldn't even be able to properly
label a diagram of my organs
think of me that way too
and would give me no choice
but to birth babies I never wanted.
I am a person, not a bitch who exists
to fulfill your breeding kinks
and pregnancy fetishes.
I am a human being, not an incubator.)*
This is why I had pamphlets on
short-acting, reversible, and barrier methods
of birth control thrown at me
before I was shoved out of
a male gynecologist's office at 21,
even though I was abstinent,
certain, and begging

At a hospital, when my mother
stepped out of the room,
another male gynecologist
had me spread my legs for him

more than was necessary in
the span of my three-day stay
so he could check, and recheck, internal sutures
He took advantage of how trusting I was
of a medical professional
and how scared I was about the bleeding,
which a female gynecologist later told me was
normal to expect after a hysterectomy

I have never belonged to myself
because there has always been a man
who believes he owns me

Aego (Without the Self)

I'm easily disappointed in myself
It starts out fine
I promise I really feel fine when you ask
Better than fine even
I want to make you feel good because
you make me feel good
every way you can

When you hold me close and tell me
all of the things you love about me
When you look at me like I'm
the most beautiful thing you've ever seen
and make me feel wanted

I want to make it up to you
because there's a rope between us that
I'm always pulling on,
always taking more from you
than I'm ever able to give up
and it's not fair

I want to be a normal partner
who can share normal experiences with you
without hating myself
and being disgusted

with my body afterwards

You don't have the high expectations for me
that I've placed on my own head
like a crown of thorns
You never have any expectations for me
You tell me that I don't owe you,
that I don't need to push myself,
that you still feel loved even if
it's only kisses and touches
that don't lead to more

But the way that you're always so understanding
and patient with me
makes me want to help you more

That's how it starts,
with me genuinely wanting to show you
my love and gratitude
But after the crime,
with your sticky evidence in my hand,
my skin is crawling and I can't focus
on anything other than the bugs moving
underneath it anymore

Something about how
common and natural it is for you,
how easy it is to reach an end,
sometimes even twice,

makes me upset that I can't extend
the same vulnerability to you
like I wish I could

It is not common or natural or easy for me
and that's a deep root of frustration that
I feel for myself
I can't get out of my head enough
to just enjoy this the way I want to

And I think, maybe if I push through,
if I get over myself,
if we do this more and more,
I'll eventually start feeling okay

My Choice

You have the kind of smile that makes me
willingly abandon my dreams
Arms that are comfort and warmth
and convince me not to leave
Soft touches and sweet traces that
make my sturdy plans crumble
Careful lips with kind words
that turn my spite into rubble
Eyes that assure me I have
nothing more to prove
So between leaving or staying,
it's just you that I choose

The Things You Taught Me

It devastates me that you
were the person I learned to hate myself from
because I watched you since I was little

I noticed you
talking poorly to yourself in the mirror,
picking out only flaws to criticize and fixate on,
skipping meals to manage weight
and lying about not being hungry
over the sound of your growling stomach
while watching everyone else
eat themselves full of the food you prepared,
counting the hours since you last ate
to find out when you can let yourself eat again,
stepping on the scale at least three times a day
just in case the number changed,
and setting unrealistic goals of losing
15 pounds by the end of the week
(knowing you'll fail so you can
punish yourself with a harsher diet),
changing outfits four times
because the one you really wanted to wear
made you look big
I picked up on these habits,
adopted them too,

and I was so angry at you
for modeling self-hatred,
for passing down your body image issues
like you gave me your curly hair

But I forgave you because
you were just as much a victim of diet culture,
of this generational misery
that has afflicted only half of our family tree
because to be feminine,
you must embody grace,
and grace looks lithe

I'm sorry you learned these things first, mom
You didn't deserve to hate yourself
You didn't deserve everything
you put yourself through
to become more digestible for others
or more palatable to look at
You don't deserve to feel this ashamed
of how your body changed
after miraculously growing two children

You don't deserve to feel
like you're always taking up too much space
and need to make yourself smaller
to give the people around you elbow room
when you barely have enough room
in your shapewear to breathe

The Upbringing of Robots
and Pinned Butterflies

My empathy is masculine
I feel everything I can
for the gentle, sensitive men who
were never allowed to
as little boys,
they played with robots that destroyed cities
and were expected to become just that

I cry with the many of them
that are only now relearning how
to connect with their emotions,
and who are trying so hard
to tenderly rebuild the cities that
their fathers wrecked
we ache together at
the ridicule this apparently warrants

But my rage is feminine
I seethe for the women whose wings
are spread thin and
pinned down
like the butterflies they admired the freedom of
and tried to follow around the yard as children

I shout and scream in agony with them
as they are hurting, snapping, breaking
under the stomping metallic boots of
BattleMech men who never once questioned
why their flesh is soft under that steel casing
and who follow blindly in their fathers' heavy,
uncaring, unrelenting, unapologetic footsteps

I knew you cared about my comfort

when you turned off the lamp
and when I asked why,
you said it was because
the last time we did this,
I mentioned that I was anxious
being so on display

when I began to peel off my shirt
because you love the expanse of my skin,
but you noticed my hesitation,
grabbed my hands,
and asked if I would feel better
leaving it on that day

The Joke

Today, I made a joke about my sexuality.
It was casual, said out loud
without even a second thought given
and, later, I realized something really freeing.
You've made me feel
like I can talk lightly and out loud
about things like this
because I'm comfortable around you
in every way.

You ask, "Is this okay?"
with a soft hand on my skin.
Every time, without fail,
you carefully observe my reactions
"Am I being too pushy? You'd tell me, right?"
You check in with me like this,
but you never are
and your hands are always
right where I want them to be.

You ask me about my experience,
encourage me to be open
and you're just as honest with me.
There are things to be taught
and learned and understood.

We both have things to teach
and learn and understand.

I'm not attracted to you
the same way you are to me,
but you make me feel like that's okay.
We have different definitions of excited,
but you know my lack of definition
isn't a reflection of you.
You know it's just a part of me,
like the allo part of you, that simply is.

You've normalized something between us,
a topic that I used to be ashamed of,
self-conscious about.
I don't feel guilty or embarrassed
to tell you these things
like I worried I would be for a long time.

One.

But it's not their business
when they ask for my body count
I'm no more or less worth dignity
whatever the amount

The clothes that make me confident
also make me "for the street"
"A pump and dump" is all I am,
"A horny bitch in heat"

Because no "self-respecting man" would
let me post pics wearing that
Except, mine isn't so insecure
that he's got to "control his brat"

Electively carving out my womb
just proves that I'm a slut
I wouldn't be scared if I knew
it's cheaper to keep one's legs shut

a gender

I've tried not wearing makeup,
tried binding and wearing baggy,
formless clothes,
tried to deepen my voice and rid myself
of all typically feminine self-expression,
I've even tried chopping off all my hair
to see if it would make any difference,
but I've noticed that
people assign gender to me more
when I make the effort
to appear as genderless as possible

It's like they see me trying to be less *woman*,
more androgynous
and feel the need to remind me that I am always
a
girl, girl, girl
in their eyes

Why did I care?
I was trying to pass as something
outside of the gender binary
to ignorant people who would clock me
as one thing or another
no matter what I did

I was still squeezing myself into a small box
I was still trying so hard to somehow conform
What the fuck
should non-binary look like anyway
and why couldn't it look like me, just as I was?
There is no joy in existing to please others

I really am thankful for
the few people who really see me
and give me the room to express
the 'feminine' things I really enjoy,
who make me feel good about myself when
I wear that makeup and
those tight, pretty dresses,
who gave me the permission I needed
(or wanted)
to exist in my own, curvy body,
and who celebrate the euphoric experiences
I share with them in my high voice,
without projecting roles and presumptions
onto me for doing so

They laughed.

No one thought I would do it
when I told them I was planning to leave
because that would be such
a big, daring adventure
for such a small, insignificant person to go on
"Aim lower," they said to me in different words

And I listened
I didn't leave,
but a spiteful part of me really wishes I did
so I could have proved them wrong
I'm angry at myself for being scared
and sticking to familiar routines

I don't tell them my dreams now
because hoping for the future I want out loud
feels like giving them the chance
to be right again,
it feels like solidifying a goal
that I'll let myself down and never reach

Organized Manipulation

I was raised to celebrate a human sacrifice
(How strange a concept is that really?)
I was a malleable kid and was told that
my soul was saved because
a supposedly omnipotent,
all-powerful father watched
as he let his only son die gruesomely and
needlessly for me to live eternally
(Don't I feel guilty enough about this death
to stay in the religion?)
If I just accept that someone died for me,
I can spend forever worshiping the narcissist that
sent him to the cross,
who created humans in the first place,
gave them free will,
and told him to love him or else be damned
(Aren't I lucky?
Isn't having the option of going to heaven
so generous and appealing?)

I was taught to pray to a god I couldn't
see or prove the existence of
and bring tithe offerings to
the greedy human representatives
of that being every week

I watched my parents stress over money
and stretch themselves thin to make ends meet
My mother worked two jobs just to pay for
my father's life-prolonging medication
while our church happily ate
our ten percent faith tax

A spiritual man attempted to groom me
and no one did a thing about it
everyone still welcomed him and his outlandish,
so obviously untrue stories
about the fascinating miracles
god let him perform
I sat across the room from him in group studies
until I became so uncomfortable that
I just stopped going
and isolated myself from my peers
It didn't matter
because I could never seem to
relate to them anyway

I couldn't make myself cry
like they could during worship
I wasn't feeling enough
while I sang on the worship team,
I wasn't showing enough emotion
(Why didn't I feel what I was supposed to?)
And while everyone nodded in agreement
to the pastor's condemning words

during the sermon,
I felt the terror of somehow
being seen transparently
and having my own sins be exposed
I felt the burden of their
misdirected anger and hatred
Those lectures rammed against the door
of the closet I had to lock myself in to stay safe,
threatening to break it down and drag me out
and down into the depths of hell

Why does god have a
drastically higher kill count
than the devil?
For a book about good vs. evil,
it's really hard to distinguish
who's really supposed to be good
and who's supposed to be evil in the Bible
(I had too many doubts
I asked too many questions
Why was I even there if I didn't agree?)
I stopped asking for help when I was
struggling with my faith
and simply let myself lose it
When I stopped attending church,
It was like I stopped existing to
the people I had grown up with
Even family members iced me out

Organized religion is
an emotionally manipulative partner
that traps you
in an abusive, exploitative relationship
It plays off of your fears,
demands that you give your everything to it
and punishes you for even considering leaving,
for not being as devoted to it as you should be
And there's something wrong with *you*
if you aren't happy with it,
if you hate yourself when you're with it,
if you can't keep your feelings for it alive
while it mistreats you

Burn the Witch for Practicing Self-Care

My conservative father,
of a Pennsylvania Dutch
and Mennonite background
should know he has witchcraft in his heritage
He says magic is a gift from
a devil I don't believe in,
like his grandparents and his lineage before that
don't have a history
full of faith healing, folk magick,
and creating herbal remedies
Like they didn't practice
braucherei and hexerei,
or paint protection and abundance sigils
on their barns and carve them into furniture
Like they didn't have their endless superstitions
or carry enchanted stones
and other blessed items,
or believe in the power of the moon
during different phases,
or let sun zodiac signs dictate when they
should have children and plant certain crops

My Irish mother with her Catholic upbringing

should recognize how witchcraft has been
stitched into her entire rearing
She can't understand my practices
like her blessings and curses are all
just meant to be empty words
Like we don't keep Celtic symbols
in every room of our house
Like her parents' church services aren't full
of Latin chants, hymns, invocations,
and incantations,
like they don't keep a shrine in their home
with candles, religious books,
and small glass statues
of their patron saints and angels,
like their rosaries, holy water and worry stones
aren't also alter tools
Like they don't drink
symbolic blood from chalices
and cleanse their metaphorical loaf of flesh with
incense every week
or anoint themselves with oils and ashes
Like they don't have a wall in their living room
dedicated to photos of their passed ancestors
or have Samhain, Imbolc, Bealtaine and
Lughnasa marked on their calendars

My body positive affirmations
and glamour magick,
anxiety reducing tarot cartomancy,

and calming tea leaf divinations
are evil though, as if my practices
are somehow any different
than what they're used to seeing just because
I call on, *rely on* my own energy
rather than a deity's,
just because it falls under a different name
Heritage and faith. Catholicism. Witchcraft.
The devil is tricking me
onto a path of self-destruction
away from the presence of
a god I also don't believe in
and wouldn't want to be in the presence of
even if I did
Walking away from the church was
selfish and egotistical of me
I have to laugh because
they call me a pagan for the things I do,
but I just call it self-care

The Joy in Finding an Inherently Evil Place of Conceit (1 Corinthians 3:16)

I've never liked church,
a building full of holier-than-thou people
who put on a weekly performance
as characters who lead perfect lives.
They leave this facade at the door,
the same way they leave the pastor's message, -
yet another sermon about
being a light for others
in an otherwise dark world, -
just to go commit their weekly sins
where a minister isn't there
to see and rebuke their acts.
Their marks on the world are
just as filthy and sooted as anyone else's,
though they think their slates are wiped clean for
the belief they have,
that their faith excuses their behavior.
At the end of the day,
they're going to heaven
if they just believe in Jesus.
It doesn't matter what they've done.
But they seem to think they're a special case

because they're so quick
to condemn everyone else.

I've never liked church,
where the elders insist
that community and accountability are vital
for maintaining a strong faith.
Accountability, put plainly,
means being expected to confess
your guilts, shames, and shortcomings
to people who will not extend
the same vulnerability to you,
who will instead offer you
unsolicited advice, insincere prayers,
and send you on your way with a verse
that's only sort of relevant to your struggles.
James 1:3. Proverbs 3:5-6.

I've never liked church,
so I stopped going
as soon as I had the autonomy to decide not to.
I'm feeling more in touch with my spirituality
than I ever have
in the small Mennonite sanctuary
where I sat, second row from the front
and two seats in from the left-most aisle,
with my family every Sunday
for the first eighteen years of my life.
For the first time,

I feel connected to a higher power
and want to build a relationship with them.
I believe in a god,
but not the one I was raised to.
I believe in a god that believes in me too.

Church taught me never to trust myself
because I was born inherently evil.
(Does religion really need to
infect you with a disease
in order to sell you its cure?
Does it need to instill the fear of
eternal damnation in you
to stay relevant in your life?)
But as I've been doing work
to better understand myself,
I don't feel evil and untrustworthy.
There's a certain empowerment that comes
with finding the good and the divine in myself,
with finding answers in the comfort of solitude
and with the absence of
a congregation of hypocritical people
who would only judge and
label me as a self-absorbed,
misguided sinner for doing so.
I've come to find that I am a place of worship
that is deserving of love and grace.
I am a holy spirit.
1 Corinthians 3:16.

Vessel of Want (human)

I hate thinking of myself as a sexual vessel
in any capacity
It's humiliating when my libido flares,
when I feel needy and *want, want, want*
(so selfishly, the way I was taught not to)
the things that I hate imagining for myself,
things that fill me with disgust any other day,
only because
it's *me,*

But you don't judge me for wanting
you show me love instead and
give me all I ask for,
more than I ask for
You tell me I'm enough,
and do your best to make me feel human
to combat the way my shame makes me feel

Healing and Guilt

Healing is hard
when your progress is so quickly
undoing the rewards of your suffering

I gave several years of my life,
a decade, to be exact
to an eating disorder

What was it all for if getting better
means gaining back the weight
I hurt myself to lose?

When the promise I made to myself
on ribs that used to be visible
reminds me of the addictive control I now lack
over my body
every time I see it?

I can't explain that sense of loss to anyone
or how guilty I feel towards my teenage self
for what I put them through
every time I finish a full meal

Still Wearing a Mask

My masking didn't end
when everyone else took theirs off.
I've worn one for most of my life and
I still wear one to work every day,
to every social event I attend.

Before I even start my day,
I practice all the conversations
I expect to have,
or worry I might have,
with myself in the shower.
I write scripts for myself and act them out.

My lines prove useful
when I'm later trapped in conversation.
I force uncomfortable eye contact
because it would be rude if I didn't.

I mirror facial expressions
to match the energy of the people I talk to
because otherwise, I have RBF.
(How do people naturally smile for that long?
My cheeks hurt.)

I imitate their tones and inflections

so I don't sound bored by what they're saying,
even if I am
draining myself with small talk.

I don't care how your weekend was,
but it's polite to ask and grin as you go
on and on about your family's barbecue
and how lucky you were that
the weather was nice.
(God, will someone please just talk to me
about their favorite childhood memories,
their biggest fears,
or deep-rooted trauma for once?)

I don't bounce in place
or make sounds like I want to
and I don't relate what you just said to
a quote from my favorite TV show
(which I've rewatched all 15 seasons of
12 times now)
in order to connect with you.

When I blink too much because of the
bright fluorescent lights,
I play it off like I have something in my eye.
I do not scratch my skin raw when
the tag in my shirt is itching
or take off my shoes when
I feel the unbearable seams

of my socks on my toes.

I shake your hand even though
I'm wondering when
the last time you washed it was
and how many door handles
you've touched since then.
(I don't want to be touched.)

I don't put in earbuds when
your open-mouthed gum-chewing and
the hum of the air conditioner and
the buzz of electric and
the background conversations of other people
overlapping the sound of music
playing from somewhere
becomes too much.

And I put a lid on the simmering pot.
I'll let it boil over only when I get home
so I don't cause a public scene
and embarrass myself.

I'm still masking and it's hard to breathe.

Write What You Know

There are certain people who
I hope never discover my posted work
I hope they never find out
I've written about them
and what they put me through
because I don't want to give them
the satisfaction
of reading about how much they hurt me
I don't want them to know that
I still think about what they've done

But then, there are people in my life who
inspire themes of healing and growth
And when I send them links,
I wonder if they can see themselves
in what they've read,
if they pick up on just how often
I write pieces of them into my stories,
how often the characters they inspired
are somehow loving and so caring towards
the very unlovable, fragile, broken ones
I projected myself onto
I hope I worded
my appreciation towards them well
I hope they receive the message

that I'm always grateful
for all the times they let me
be myself around them
and how they've accepted me anyway,
encouraged me

Are they reading between
the lines of my writing
and seeing how many love letters
are meant for them?